Ant Farm Mastery: A Step-by-Step Guide to Creating and Maintaining Your Own Ant Colony

Contents

Chapters:

1. **Introduction to Ant Farming**
   - Understanding the Fascination with Ant Farms
   - Benefits of Building Your Own Ant Farm

2. **Getting to Know Your Ants**
   - Common Ant Species for Ant Farms
   - Understanding Ant Behavior and Social Structure

3. **Designing Your Ant Farm**
   - Choosing the Right Type of Ant Farm (Traditional, Gel, DIY, etc.)
   - Key Elements of a Successful Ant Farm Design

4. **Gathering Materials and Tools**
   - Essential Equipment and Supplies
   - Where to Source Your Ant Colony

5. **Building the Foundation**
   - Step-by-Step Guide to Assembling Your Ant Farm
   - Preparing the Environment for Your Ants

6. **Introducing Ants to Their New Home**

- Safe Transport and Introduction of Your Ant Colony
- Ensuring a Smooth Transition for Your Ants

7. **Maintaining a Healthy Ant Farm**
    - Feeding and Hydration Guidelines
    - Cleaning and Care Tips for Long-Term Success

8. **Troubleshooting Common Issues**
    - Addressing Escapees and Structural Problems
    - Dealing with Sick or Unhealthy Ants

9. **Advanced Ant Farming Techniques**
    - Expanding and Modifying Your Ant Farm
    - Breeding and Colony Growth Strategies

10. **Sharing Your Ant Farm with Others**
    - Educating Friends and Family About Your Ant Farm
    - Participating in Ant Farming Communities

11. **Conclusion**
    - Reflecting on Your Ant Farming Journey
    - The Future of Your Ant Colony and Next Steps

This structure provides a comprehensive guide, making it accessible for beginners while also offering advanced tips for more experienced enthusiasts.

Chapter 1: Introduction to Ant Farming

Ant farming is an intriguing hobby that has captivated people of all ages for centuries. In this chapter, we'll delve into the origins of ant farming, exploring how it has evolved from a simple pastime to a popular educational tool and hobby. By understanding the history and appeal of ant farming, you'll gain a deeper appreciation for why these tiny creatures have captured the fascination of so many.

The History of Ant Farming

The concept of keeping ants in a controlled environment dates back to the early 20th century when the first commercial ant farms were introduced. These early versions were simple glass or plastic containers filled with sand or soil, allowing people to observe ants in their natural habitat. Over time, as our understanding of ants grew, so did the complexity and design of ant farms. Today, modern ant farms offer a variety of features, including intricate tunnels, feeding stations, and even digital monitoring systems.

The Appeal of Ant Farming

What makes ant farming so appealing? For many, it's the opportunity to observe the complex social structures and behaviors of ants up close. Ants are known for their remarkable teamwork, with each member of the colony playing a specific role, from workers to soldiers to the queen. Watching ants work together to build tunnels, gather food, and care for their young can be both mesmerizing and educational.

Ant farming also offers a unique connection to nature, providing a window into the often-overlooked world of insects. Unlike traditional pets, ants require minimal maintenance and space, making them an ideal choice for people with busy lifestyles or limited living space.

The Benefits of Building and Maintaining an Ant Farm

Creating and maintaining an ant farm isn't just a fun activity—it also comes with a host of benefits. For children and adults alike, ant farms can serve as a powerful educational tool. They offer insights into biology, ecology, and the importance of cooperation. Ant farms can also help cultivate a sense of responsibility and curiosity, encouraging individuals to learn more about the natural world.

Beyond education, ant farming brings simple joy. The act of setting up an ant farm, observing the ants' progress, and watching the colony grow can be a soothing and rewarding experience. It's a hobby that fosters patience, observation skills, and an appreciation for the small wonders of life.

In this chapter, you've been introduced to the fascinating world of ant farming. As we move forward, you'll learn how to create your own ant farm, care for your ants, and explore the many ways this hobby can enrich your life.

Chapter 2: Getting to Know Your Ants

Before you embark on the journey of building an ant farm, it's essential to familiarize yourself with the fascinating world of ants. Understanding the species you're going to care for is the key to creating a thriving and sustainable environment for them. This chapter will guide you through the different ant species that are well-suited for ant farming, exploring their behaviors, social structures, and the specific roles each ant plays within the colony.

Understanding Ant Species

Not all ants are the same, and each species has its own unique traits that make them either suitable or unsuitable for an ant farm. In this section, we'll explore some of the most popular ant species commonly kept in ant farms:

1. **Harvester Ants (Pogonomyrmex spp.):**
    - **Behavior:** Known for their industrious nature, harvester ants are efficient foragers. They collect seeds, which they store and use as food.
    - **Social Structure:** Like most ants, harvester ants have a clear social hierarchy, with a queen, workers, and sometimes soldiers.

- **Role in the Colony:** Workers are responsible for gathering food, tending to the queen and brood, and maintaining the nest. Soldiers, if present, protect the colony from threats.

2. **Carpenter Ants (Camponotus spp.):**
    - **Behavior:** Carpenter ants are large and known for their wood-boring habits in nature, though they won't damage your ant farm. They are active foragers and can be fascinating to observe.
    - **Social Structure:** These ants also have a clear division of labor, with workers, a queen, and sometimes soldiers.
    - **Role in the Colony:** Workers care for the young, gather food, and protect the queen. They are also responsible for building and maintaining the nest.

3. **Field Ants (Formica spp.):**
    - **Behavior:** Field ants are common in many regions and are known for their adaptability. They can forage for a variety of foods, making them easy to care for.
    - **Social Structure:** Field ants have a typical ant social structure with workers, a queen, and soldiers.

- **Role in the Colony:** Workers are versatile, tending to the queen and brood, gathering food, and defending the nest.

4. **Lasius Niger (Black Garden Ant):**
    - **Behavior:** These ants are hardy and adaptable, making them one of the most popular choices for ant farms. They thrive in various environments and are easy to care for.
    - **Social Structure:** The social structure includes a queen and a large number of workers.
    - **Role in the Colony:** Workers are responsible for feeding the colony, caring for the queen and young, and maintaining the nest structure.

Ant Behavior and Social Structures

Ants are social insects, and their colonies operate with a high degree of organization and cooperation. Understanding the social structure of your chosen species is vital:

- **The Queen:** The queen is the most important member of the colony. Her primary role is to reproduce, ensuring the survival and growth of the colony. She is usually larger than the workers and can live for several years.
- **Workers:** These ants are the backbone of the colony. They are responsible for foraging for food, caring for the queen and her brood, and maintaining the nest. Workers

are sterile females and make up the majority of the colony.

- **Soldiers (if present):** In some species, soldiers are specialized workers with larger mandibles, designed to defend the colony from predators or other threats. Not all ant species have a distinct soldier caste.

- **Brood (Larvae and Pupae):** The young ants in the colony, which the workers diligently care for. They are fed and protected until they mature into adult ants.

Choosing the Right Species for Your Ant Farm

When selecting a species for your ant farm, consider the following factors:

- **Environmental Needs:** Some species require specific temperature and humidity levels. Make sure your ant farm can accommodate these needs.

- **Colony Size:** Different species have varying colony sizes. Ensure that your farm has enough space to support the growth of the colony.

- **Food Preferences:** Some ants are specialized in their diet, such as seed-eating harvester ants, while others are generalists. Choose a species that matches the type of food you can readily provide.

- **Activity Level:** Some ants are more active and interesting to observe than others. If you're looking for an ant farm that provides a lot of activity, choose a species known for its industrious behavior.

By the end of this chapter, you'll have a thorough understanding of the different species of ants and their unique characteristics. This knowledge will empower you to make an informed decision when choosing the species that will thrive in your ant farm. With the right species, your ant farm will not only be a thriving habitat but also a source of endless fascination and learning.

Chapter 3: Designing Your Ant Farm

Designing your ant farm is a crucial step that can determine the overall success and enjoyment of your ant-keeping experience. This chapter will guide you through the different types of ant farms, highlighting the strengths and weaknesses of each, so you can choose the one that best suits your needs and preferences.

1. Traditional Glass Setups

Traditional glass ant farms are classic and elegant, providing a clear view of the ants as they tunnel through the substrate. These setups typically consist of two glass panes held together with a narrow space in between for the ants to build their tunnels.

Pros:

- **Excellent Visibility:** Glass offers a clear and unobstructed view of the ants and their intricate tunnels, making it easy to observe their behavior.
- **Aesthetic Appeal:** Glass farms often look more polished and can be displayed as a decorative piece in your home.
- **Durability:** Glass is a long-lasting material that won't easily scratch or wear down over time.

Cons:

- **Fragility:** Glass can break if dropped or mishandled, posing a risk to both the ants and the keeper.
- **Weight:** Glass farms can be heavier and more cumbersome to move around.
- **Temperature Sensitivity:** Glass can conduct heat, which may require careful placement to avoid overheating the ants.

2. Gel Farms

Gel ant farms are a modern alternative to traditional setups, featuring a clear gel that doubles as both a habitat and a food source for the ants. This design eliminates the need for regular feeding and watering, making it a low-maintenance option.

Pros:

- **Low Maintenance:** The gel provides both nutrition and hydration, significantly reducing the upkeep required.
- **Ease of Use:** Gel farms are often marketed as beginner-friendly, with a simple setup process.
- **Clear View:** The transparent gel allows for easy observation of the ants as they dig tunnels.

Cons:

- **Limited Longevity:** Once the gel is consumed or dries out, it cannot be replaced, limiting the lifespan of the farm.

- **Artificial Environment:** The gel doesn't mimic the ants' natural environment, which can affect their behavior and well-being.
- **Limited Species Suitability:** Not all ant species will thrive in a gel farm, making it less versatile.

3. DIY Ant Farms

For those who enjoy a hands-on approach, creating a DIY ant farm can be a rewarding project. DIY farms can be customized to suit your specific needs and can be made from a variety of materials, such as acrylic, plastic containers, or even old picture frames.

Pros:

- **Customizability:** You can design the farm to your exact specifications, including size, shape, and materials.
- **Cost-Effective:** DIY options are often more affordable, as you can repurpose materials you already have.
- **Educational:** Building your own ant farm can be a great learning experience, helping you understand the needs and behaviors of ants more deeply.

Cons:

- **Time-Consuming:** Building a farm from scratch requires time and effort, which might not be ideal for everyone.

- **Potential for Mistakes:** Without proper planning, a DIY farm could have design flaws that affect the ants' environment and health.

- **Material Quality:** Depending on the materials used, DIY farms might not be as durable or safe as professionally made options.

4. Key Elements of a Thriving Ant Environment

Regardless of the type of ant farm you choose, certain elements are essential for creating a thriving environment for your ants:

- **Proper Ventilation:** Ensure that your ant farm has adequate airflow to prevent mold growth and maintain a healthy environment.

- **Moisture Control:** Ants require a certain level of humidity to thrive, so it's important to regulate moisture levels in the farm.

- **Escape Prevention:** Make sure that your ant farm is securely sealed to prevent any unwanted escapes.

- **Suitable Substrate:** The substrate is the material in which the ants will tunnel. For traditional farms, sand, soil, or a combination of both can be used. The substrate should be non-toxic and free of contaminants.

- **Temperature Regulation:** Keep your ant farm in a stable environment, away from direct sunlight or cold drafts, to maintain the ideal temperature for your ants.

By carefully considering these design options and elements, you'll be well on your way to creating an ant farm that is both functional and visually appealing. Whether you choose a traditional glass setup, a gel farm, or a DIY project, the design you select will set the foundation for your ants' happiness and health.

Chapter 4: Gathering Materials and Tools

Building an ant farm is a rewarding project that requires careful preparation. Before you can start assembling your ant farm, you'll need to gather all the necessary materials and tools. This chapter is dedicated to providing you with a detailed guide on what you'll need, ensuring that you're fully equipped to create a thriving environment for your ants.

1. Basic Components of an Ant Farm

- **Container:** The primary component of your ant farm is the container where the ants will live. It can be made of glass, acrylic, or plastic. The size and shape will depend on the design you've chosen, but it should be transparent so you can observe the ants. Common choices include:
    - **Glass or Acrylic Aquarium:** Provides a sturdy, transparent enclosure with ample space.
    - **Plastic Containers:** More lightweight and affordable, though they may scratch easily.
- **Substrate:** This is the material that lines the bottom of the farm, providing a natural environment for the ants. Sand, soil, or a mix of both are commonly used. The substrate should be sterile and free of chemicals or pesticides.

- **Nest Area:** Some designs require a dedicated nesting area where the queen and workers can establish their colony. This can be made from plaster, gypsum, or other materials that retain moisture.
- **Lid or Cover:** To prevent escapes, your ant farm will need a secure lid. It should be breathable but escape-proof, often made from mesh or a perforated material.

2. Tools for Assembly

- **Cutting Tools:** Depending on the materials you're using, you may need a variety of cutting tools:
    - **Glass Cutter:** For shaping glass containers.
    - **Utility Knife or Scissors:** For cutting plastic or other softer materials.
    - **Dremel Tool or Rotary Cutter:** Useful for precise cuts, especially with acrylic or more complex designs.
- **Adhesives and Sealants:** To assemble the various parts of your ant farm, you'll need strong, non-toxic adhesives.
    - **Silicone Sealant:** Ideal for sealing glass or acrylic.
    - **Epoxy Resin:** For more durable bonds, particularly in intricate designs.
- **Measuring Tools:** Accurate measurements ensure a well-constructed ant farm.

- **Ruler or Tape Measure:** Essential for marking dimensions.
- **Level:** To ensure your ant farm is perfectly horizontal, preventing any lopsidedness.

3. Specialized Equipment for Advanced Designs

- **Heating Element:** If you live in a cooler climate, you might need to maintain a consistent temperature within the ant farm. A small heating pad or cable can be used, placed under or around the container.
- **Humidity Control:** For species that require a specific humidity level, you may need a hygrometer to monitor moisture levels and a humidifier to maintain them.
- **Ant Feeding Tools:** Specialized tools, such as feeding dishes or tubes, help provide food and water without disturbing the colony.

4. Sourcing Your Ant Colony

Once your ant farm is ready, you'll need to introduce a colony. Here are the most common ways to source ants:

- **Purchasing Ants Online:** Many reputable suppliers offer various ant species, complete with a queen and workers. This option ensures you receive a healthy, established colony.

- **Capturing Ants in the Wild:** If you're adventurous and patient, you can capture a queen during the nuptial flight season. This method requires careful handling and a good understanding of local ant species.

- **Receiving Ants from a Fellow Enthusiast:** If you know someone who keeps ants, they might be willing to share a portion of their colony with you.

5. Safety Considerations

While gathering materials, it's crucial to consider safety. Wear gloves when handling adhesives and cutting tools, and work in a well-ventilated area when using chemicals. Always ensure that the materials you use are non-toxic and safe for both you and the ants.

Chapter 5: Building the Foundation

With your materials ready, it's time to start building your ant farm. This chapter provides a detailed, step-by-step guide to assembling your ant farm, ensuring that every crucial step is covered. Whether you're a beginner or have some experience, these instructions will help you create a stable, functional environment for your ants.

Step 1: Assembling the Basic Structure

1. **Choosing the Container:** Start by selecting the right container for your ant farm. This could be a glass or plastic enclosure, such as a fish tank, a custom-built acrylic farm, or even a DIY setup. The container should be transparent so you can observe the ants, and it must have a secure lid to prevent escape.

2. **Creating a Framework:** If your container doesn't come with built-in dividers, you'll need to create them. These dividers can be made from acrylic sheets, plastic, or even wood. The goal is to create vertical chambers where ants can dig and create tunnels. Secure these dividers firmly to the base and sides of the container using non-toxic glue.

3. **Ventilation:** Drill or cut small holes in the lid or sides of the container for ventilation. The holes should be small enough to prevent ants from escaping but large enough

to allow air circulation. Cover these holes with a fine mesh if necessary.

Step 2: Preparing the Substrate

1. **Choosing the Right Substrate:** The substrate is the material your ants will dig through to create their tunnels. Common choices include sand, soil, or a mix of both. Some ant keepers prefer a layered approach, with sand on top and soil beneath. The substrate should be clean and free from contaminants.

2. **Layering the Substrate:** Pour the substrate into the container, filling it to a depth of about 2 to 4 inches (5 to 10 cm), depending on the size of the container and the species of ants you're keeping. Lightly pack the substrate down to create a firm base for the ants to start digging.

3. **Moisture Management:** Maintaining the right level of moisture in the substrate is crucial for the ants' survival. Some ant species prefer a dry environment, while others need a humid one. Use a spray bottle to mist the substrate lightly, ensuring it's moist but not waterlogged. You can insert a moisture gradient by dampening only one side of the substrate, giving the ants the option to choose their preferred humidity level.

Step 3: Setting Up the Environment

1. **Temperature Control:** Most ants thrive at temperatures between 70°F and 80°F (21°C to 27°C). If you live in a cooler climate, consider using a heat mat or lamp to maintain a consistent temperature within the enclosure. Place the heat source on one side of the container to create a temperature gradient.

2. **Lighting:** Ants are sensitive to light, so keep the ant farm in a dimly lit area. If you want to observe your ants without disturbing them, use a red LED light, as ants cannot see red light, and it won't affect their behavior.

3. **Adding Decoration and Hiding Spots:** While not essential, adding small decorations like rocks, twigs, or leaves can make the environment more natural and aesthetically pleasing. These elements can also provide hiding spots for the ants and encourage natural behavior.

Step 4: Final Checks and Adjustments

1. **Safety Check:** Before introducing your ants, ensure that the container is secure, with no gaps or loose parts that could allow the ants to escape. Double-check the ventilation holes and lid for any weaknesses.

2. **Humidity and Temperature Monitoring:** Use a hygrometer and thermometer to monitor the conditions inside the ant farm. Adjust the moisture level and temperature as needed, ensuring that everything is within the ideal range for your ant species.

3. **Observation Window:** If your container is not entirely transparent, consider creating an observation window by placing a clear acrylic sheet against one side of the substrate. This will allow you to observe the ants' tunneling behavior without disturbing them.

By the end of this chapter, you'll have a fully assembled ant farm ready to welcome its new inhabitants. With the foundation laid, your ants will have a comfortable, safe environment to explore and thrive in.

Chapter 6: Introducing Ants to Their New Home

Introducing ants to their new habitat is one of the most crucial steps in establishing a thriving ant farm. This process requires not only careful handling but also an understanding of the ants' behavior and needs during this transition. In this chapter, we will guide you through every step of the introduction process, from preparing the ant farm to monitoring the ants' adjustment to their new environment.

Preparing the Ant Farm

Before introducing your ants, it's essential to ensure that their new home is ready and optimized for their needs. Here's what you need to do:

- **Temperature and Humidity**: Ensure that the ant farm is at the right temperature and humidity levels. Ants are sensitive to environmental changes, and the wrong conditions can cause stress.

- **Nest Area Preparation**: If your farm has a designated nesting area, make sure it's moist and dark. Ants prefer these conditions when settling into a new home.

- **Food and Water**: Place small amounts of food and a water source in the farm. This will encourage the ants to explore and feel comfortable in their new surroundings.

- **Safety Check**: Inspect the farm for any sharp edges, gaps, or loose parts that could harm the ants or allow them to escape.

Transporting the Ants

The journey from their current location to the new ant farm can be stressful for the ants. Follow these steps to ensure a smooth and safe transport:

- **Use the Right Container**: If your ants are currently in a temporary container, ensure it is secure and well-ventilated for transport.
- **Minimize Handling**: Avoid handling the ants directly. Instead, gently coax them into a container using a soft brush or by tilting their current habitat.
- **Keep the Container Stable**: During transport, keep the container steady and avoid sudden movements. Ants can become agitated by excessive shaking or vibrations.

Introducing the Ants

Once your ants have arrived at their new home, the introduction should be done gradually to minimize stress:

- **Gradual Release**: Open the transport container inside the ant farm and allow the ants to exit at their own pace. Avoid forcing them out, as this can cause panic.

- **Monitor Behavior**: Observe the ants as they explore their new environment. Signs of a successful introduction include the ants calmly exploring the farm, finding food, and beginning to dig or settle into the nest area.

- **Avoid Disturbance**: After the initial introduction, minimize disturbances for the next few hours. This allows the ants to acclimate to their new surroundings without additional stress.

Monitoring the Adjustment Period

The first few days after introducing the ants are critical for their long-term success in the farm. Pay close attention to the following:

- **Activity Levels**: Healthy ants will be active, exploring their environment, and interacting with each other. If the ants seem lethargic or disoriented, it may indicate stress or environmental issues.

- **Nesting Behavior**: Look for signs that the ants are beginning to establish a nest. This could involve digging tunnels or gathering in a specific area of the farm.

- **Feeding Habits**: Ensure that the ants are finding and consuming the food you've provided. A lack of interest in food could be a sign of stress or poor health.

- **Communication**: Ants communicate through pheromones. Watch for ants following each other or clustering together, which indicates that they are sharing information and working as a colony.

Troubleshooting Common Issues

If the ants are not adjusting well, there are a few common issues to consider:

- **Environmental Conditions**: Double-check the temperature, humidity, and light levels. Even small deviations can cause problems.

- **Farm Design**: Ensure that the design of the farm allows the ants to feel secure. If the farm is too open or lacks proper nesting areas, the ants may struggle to settle.

- **Health of the Colony**: Sometimes, issues with adjustment can be due to the health of the ants. If you notice any unusual behavior or appearance, consider consulting with an expert or researching further.

By following these guidelines, you'll create a smooth transition for your ants as they settle into their new home. Proper introduction sets the foundation for a thriving ant farm, where your colony can grow and flourish in a safe and supportive environment.

Chapter 7: Maintaining a Healthy Ant Farm

A thriving ant farm isn't just about setting it up and watching the ants go about their business; it requires ongoing care and attention. In this chapter, we'll delve into the essential practices that ensure your ant colony remains healthy, active, and content in their environment.

1. Feeding Your Ants

Proper nutrition is the foundation of a healthy ant farm. Ants require a balanced diet that typically consists of:

- **Sugars:** Ants need sugars for energy. You can provide them with honey, sugar water, or fruit like apples or grapes. Be sure to remove any uneaten fruit before it starts to spoil.

- **Proteins:** Protein is crucial for the growth and development of the colony, particularly for the queen and the larvae. You can feed your ants small pieces of insect meat, such as crushed crickets or mealworms, or protein-rich foods like egg yolk or commercial ant food.

- **Water:** Hydration is critical, but ants can drown easily, so it's important to provide water in a way that's safe for them. A piece of water-soaked cotton ball or a sponge can serve as a water source.

Feeding Schedule: Establishing a regular feeding schedule will help maintain the health and vigor of your ants. Depending on the species and the size of your colony, you may need to feed them every day or every few days. Be observant of how much food is consumed and adjust accordingly. Overfeeding can lead to mold and pests, while underfeeding can weaken the colony.

2. Hydration Techniques

Just like all living creatures, ants need a constant supply of water. However, providing water requires care to avoid accidents:

- **Moisture Control:** Keep the farm's substrate slightly moist to simulate their natural environment. This can be done by lightly spraying the substrate with water using a spray bottle.
- **Direct Water Supply:** As mentioned earlier, a damp cotton ball or a sponge works well. Replace it regularly to prevent mold growth.

Monitor Moisture Levels: Different ant species have varying moisture needs, so it's essential to research the specific requirements of your colony. Too much moisture can cause the growth of harmful fungi, while too little can lead to dehydration.

3. Maintaining Cleanliness

A clean environment is vital for the health of your ant farm. Ants, like all insects, produce waste, which, if not managed, can lead to unsanitary conditions and diseases. Here's how to keep the farm clean:

- **Waste Management:** Ants typically create a "trash pile" where they deposit waste and food remains. Periodically remove this waste to keep the farm clean. Use a small, gentle brush or tweezers to do this.
- **Cleaning the Farm:** Over time, the glass or plastic walls of the ant farm can become smeared or dirty. Carefully clean the inside of the walls without disturbing the colony. A damp cloth can be used to wipe down the walls.

Regular Inspections: Regularly inspect your ant farm for signs of mold, pests, or excessive waste buildup. If you notice any issues, address them promptly to prevent them from affecting the colony.

4. Handling Routine Maintenance

Routine maintenance tasks are necessary to ensure the long-term success of your ant farm. Here are some tips:

- **Substrate Replacement:** Depending on the species and the farm's design, you may need to replace the substrate (the material the ants tunnel through) occasionally. This is a delicate process that requires temporarily moving the ants to a different container.

- **Humidity and Temperature Control:** Keep the environment within the ideal range for your ant species. Use a hygrometer and thermometer to monitor conditions, and make adjustments as needed.

Preventing Escape: While performing maintenance, be mindful of preventing escapes. Ants are small and quick, so always close the farm securely after completing any task.

Conclusion

By following the guidelines in this chapter, you'll ensure that your ant farm remains a healthy, thriving environment for your colony. Regular feeding, hydration, and cleaning are the cornerstones of successful ant farming. With careful attention to these details, your ants will continue to thrive, providing you with endless fascination and learning opportunities.

Chapter 8: Troubleshooting Common Issues

Even with the most meticulous care, issues can sometimes arise when maintaining an ant farm. This chapter is designed to help you navigate these challenges, offering solutions and preventative measures to keep your ant colony healthy and your farm in top condition.

Ants Escaping

One of the most common issues is ants escaping from the farm. This can happen for various reasons, including improper sealing, cracks in the structure, or overpopulation.

- **Identifying Escapes:** Regularly check the seals and edges of the farm for any gaps or weaknesses. If you notice ants outside their designated area, investigate immediately to find the escape route.

- **Preventing Escapes:** Ensure all seals are tight and secure. Using a thin layer of petroleum jelly around the edges can create a barrier that ants are reluctant to cross. If overpopulation is the cause, consider expanding the farm or splitting the colony.

- **Addressing Escapes:** If you find ants have already escaped, carefully collect them and return them to the farm, sealing any gaps afterward. For larger escapes, you may need to temporarily transfer the colony to a secure container while repairs are made.

Structural Issues with the Farm

Structural issues can compromise the safety and functionality of your ant farm.

- **Identifying Structural Problems:** Look out for signs such as cracks in the glass or plastic, loose joints, or warping of the materials. These can occur due to age, temperature fluctuations, or accidental damage.

- **Preventing Structural Issues:** Regular maintenance and inspections can help catch problems early. Avoid placing the farm in direct sunlight or near sources of heat to prevent warping. Handle the farm carefully to avoid accidental damage.

- **Repairing Structural Issues:** Small cracks can often be repaired with clear adhesive, but larger issues may require replacing parts of the farm. If a major structural failure occurs, temporarily rehouse the ants while making necessary repairs.

Health Problems Within the Colony

Your ants' health is critical to the success of your ant farm. Issues such as disease, parasites, or malnutrition can have severe consequences if not addressed quickly.

- **Recognizing Health Problems:** Signs of illness include lethargy, discoloration, or unusual behavior such as erratic movement. If you notice a significant number of dead ants, this could indicate a serious issue.

- **Preventing Health Problems:** Maintain a clean environment, provide a balanced diet, and avoid overcrowding. Regularly remove waste and uneaten food to prevent the buildup of harmful bacteria.

- **Addressing Health Problems:** If you suspect disease or parasites, isolate the affected ants if possible. Clean the farm thoroughly and replace the substrate if needed. In some cases, it may be necessary to consult with an expert in entomology for advice on treatment.

Handling Emergencies

In some cases, you may face more urgent situations, such as a sudden collapse of the farm structure, a severe ant escape, or a health crisis within the colony.

- **Emergency Preparedness:** Always have a backup plan, such as a temporary housing container, in case you need to move the ants quickly. Keep basic repair tools and materials on hand for quick fixes.

- **Responding to Emergencies:** Act quickly but calmly. If the structure fails, prioritize the safety of the colony and secure them in a temporary container. For health emergencies, isolate affected ants and address the issue as outlined earlier.

Making Repairs

Regular maintenance and timely repairs are essential to the longevity of your ant farm.

- **Basic Repair Techniques:** Learn how to fix minor cracks, replace broken parts, and reseal the farm. Having a repair kit with essential tools and materials like adhesive, sealant, and spare parts can be invaluable.

- **When to Seek Professional Help:** If the damage is extensive or you're unsure how to proceed, it might be best to consult a professional or consider purchasing a new farm to ensure the safety of your ants.

By being proactive and attentive, you can address these common issues effectively, ensuring that your ant farm remains a thriving and educational environment for both you and your ants.

Chapter 9: Advanced Ant Farming Techniques

1. Expanding Your Ant Farm

- **Modular Designs**: Explore modular ant farm systems that allow for easy expansion. Learn how to connect additional modules to your existing setup to accommodate a growing colony.

- **Multi-Chamber Systems**: Discover advanced setups featuring interconnected chambers to simulate a more natural habitat and provide ants with various environments to explore and utilize.

- **Vertical Expansion**: Techniques for adding vertical space, such as stacking multiple levels or using tall, narrow setups to maximize space efficiency.

2. Creating a Thriving Environment

- **Microclimate Control**: Techniques for maintaining optimal temperature, humidity, and light conditions. Invest in equipment like temperature regulators and humidity sensors to fine-tune your ant farm's environment.

- **Soil and Substrate Types**: Learn about different types of soil and substrates that can enhance ant health and activity. Understand how to prepare and maintain these materials.

3. Breeding Strategies

- **Encouraging Reproduction**: Strategies to stimulate ant reproduction, including diet enhancements, environmental adjustments, and breeding season simulation.

- **Nuptial Flights and Queen Rearing**: Learn about the natural mating processes of ants, including how to manage nuptial flights and rear new queens.

- **Egg and Larvae Care**: Best practices for handling and caring for ant eggs and larvae to ensure successful development and minimize losses.

4. Population Management

- **Colony Segregation**: Techniques for managing and splitting large colonies into smaller, more manageable groups to prevent overcrowding and reduce stress on the ants.

- **Health Monitoring**: Methods for monitoring ant health and detecting signs of disease or infestation early. Implementing regular checks and preventative measures to maintain a healthy colony.

5. Innovative Techniques

- **Artificial Nesting Materials**: Experiment with different types of artificial nesting materials to simulate natural environments and encourage different behaviors in your ants.

- **Custom Feeding Stations**: Design and implement custom feeding stations that cater to the specific dietary needs of different ant species or stages of development.

6. Troubleshooting and Problem Solving

- **Common Issues**: Address common problems that advanced ant farmers might face, such as mold growth, pest infestations, or aggressive behavior within the colony.
- **Solutions and Remedies**: Provide practical solutions and remedies to tackle these issues effectively and maintain a healthy ant farm.

7. Case Studies and Success Stories

- **Real-Life Examples**: Include case studies and success stories from experienced ant farmers who have implemented advanced techniques successfully. Learn from their experiences and apply their strategies to your own ant farm.

This chapter aims to push the boundaries of standard ant farming, offering experienced enthusiasts new challenges and creative ways to enhance their ant farms. It's designed to inspire innovation and continuous improvement in the practice of ant farming.

Chapter 10: Sharing Your Ant Farm with Others

highlights the social aspects of ant farming and how to spread your enthusiasm for this unique hobby. Here's a more detailed breakdown:

1. **Educating Others About Ant Farming:**
    - **Introduction to Ant Farming:** Explain what ant farming is and why it's fascinating. Share the basics of ant behavior, colony structure, and the benefits of observing ants.
    - **Demonstrations:** Offer tips on how to safely demonstrate ant farms to others. This could involve setting up educational displays or organizing live demonstrations in controlled environments.
    - **Safety Precautions:** Discuss the importance of handling ants with care to avoid stressing them and ensuring visitors understand not to disrupt the colony.

2. **Sharing the Joy with Friends and Family:**
    - **Invitations to Observe:** Suggest ways to invite friends and family to see your ant farm, such as hosting an "ant party" where people can learn and interact with your setup.

- **Educational Activities:** Offer ideas for activities that can help others learn more about ants, such as creating ant-themed games or quizzes.

3. **Joining Ant Farming Communities:**

    - **Online Communities:** Highlight various online forums, social media groups, and websites where ant enthusiasts gather. Explain how these platforms can provide support, share knowledge, and connect with like-minded individuals.
    - **Local Clubs and Meetups:** Encourage readers to look for or start local ant farming clubs or meetups. These can be great opportunities for hands-on learning and networking.

4. **Benefits of Community Engagement:**

    - **Knowledge Exchange:** Emphasize how sharing experiences and tips with others can enhance one's own understanding and enjoyment of ant farming.
    - **Support and Motivation:** Discuss how being part of a community can offer emotional support, motivation, and encouragement, especially when dealing with challenges or setbacks.

This chapter aims to inspire readers to not only enjoy their ant farms but also to engage with others who share their passion, thereby enriching their ant farming experience.

Chapter 11: Conclusion

In this final chapter, we will take a step back and reflect on the journey you've embarked on as an ant farmer. You began as a beginner, perhaps with some uncertainty, and now you stand as a knowledgeable and confident enthusiast, ready to embrace the complexities and rewards of ant farming.

1. **Reflection on Your Journey:**
    - **Growth and Learning:** We'll look back at the key milestones and learning experiences that have shaped your ant farming skills. This includes how your understanding of ant behavior, habitat management, and colony care has evolved.
    - **Challenges Overcome:** Reflect on the challenges you faced and how you addressed them, from initial setup issues to managing colony health. Acknowledge the persistence and problem-solving skills that have led to your current success.

2. **The Future of Your Ant Colony:**
    - **Potential Challenges:** Discuss potential future challenges such as disease outbreaks, colony expansion issues, or environmental changes. Provide strategies for anticipating and managing these challenges effectively.

- **Rewards and Benefits:** Highlight the ongoing rewards of maintaining a thriving ant colony, including the satisfaction of watching your colony grow, the joy of observing complex ant behaviors, and the educational value of your hobby.

3. **Next Steps:**

    - **Expanding Your Farm:** If you're interested in growing your ant farm, explore options for expansion. This could involve introducing new ant species, setting up additional colonies, or experimenting with different habitat designs.

    - **Starting New Projects:** For those who might want to diversify, suggest other related projects, such as creating an ant-themed educational exhibit, participating in ant farming communities, or contributing to citizen science initiatives.

    - **Ongoing Enjoyment:** Emphasize that even if you choose to maintain your current setup, there is always more to learn and enjoy. Encourage continued observation, research, and engagement with the ant farming community to keep the experience fresh and fulfilling.

4. **Dynamic and Ongoing Adventure:**

- **Endless Opportunities:** Reinforce that ant farming is not a static hobby but a dynamic one with endless opportunities for discovery and growth. Each colony is unique, and there is always something new to observe and learn.

This conclusion aims to celebrate your accomplishments, prepare you for future challenges, and inspire ongoing enthusiasm for ant farming. It's a reminder that your journey with your ant colony is an ever-evolving adventure, full of potential and excitement.

By Achraf Faster

www.ingramcontent.com/pod-product-compliance
Lightning Source LLC
Chambersburg PA
CBHW070950220526
45471CB00007B/2976